I ♥ MY CREPE MAKER

CookNation

I LOVE MY CREPE MAKER
THE ONLY CREPE MAKER RECIPE BOOK YOU'LL EVER NEED

ISBN 978-1-912155-71-2

DISCLAIMER

This book is designed to provide information on crepes that can be made using an electric crepe maker appliance and toppings and syrups using a stove top method. Some recipes may contain nuts or traces of nuts. Those suffering from any allergies associated with nuts should avoid any recipes containing nuts or nut based oils. This information is provided and sold with the knowledge that the publisher and author do not offer any legal or other professional advice. In the case of a need for any such expertise consult with the appropriate professional.

This book does not contain all information available on the subject, and other sources of recipes are available.
Every effort has been made to make this book as accurate as possible. However, there may be typographical and or content errors. Therefore, this book should serve only as a general guide and not as the ultimate source of subject information.

This book contains information that might be dated and is intended only to educate and entertain.
The author and publisher shall have no liability or responsibility to any person or entity regarding any loss or damage incurred, or alleged to have incurred, directly or indirectly, by the information contained in this book.

CONTENTS

INTRODUCTION

Crepes…. delightful French pancakes , soft, pale, delicate and frilly.

A delicious, snack, dessert or light lunch with all manner of sweet and savoury toppings, fillings and sauces to satisfy every taste and much too good to be celebrated just once a year on Shrove Tuesday.

I Love My Crepe Maker recipe selection provides a host of fun and filling toppings, stuffings and sauces to suit any mood, craving or occasion. Breakfast, snacks, lunches, sweet or savoury, veggie or meat, healthy or indulgent – there is something to cater for everyone.

Try our breakfast Apple & Maple Syrup Crepe or a lunchtime filler like Red Pesto & Pancetta or a delectable crepe with Salted Caramel Sauces to really hit the spot.

Serving up deliciously thin crepes can be a daunting task but with an electric crepe maker the process is simplified thanks to the smooth, non-stick hot plate, variable temperature settings together with spatula and wooden T-stick (this is a tool for spreading the crepe batter thinly and evenly).

All you need really worry about is the consistency of the batter and your choice of filling. I Love My Crepe Maker provides an array of fail-safe batter recipes to suit your palate and tips to help you make the perfect crepe every time.

Hints & Tips

- Always read the manufacturers instructions and guidelines for use and care.
- Wipe the surface of the crepe maker before use.
- Always make sure your crepe maker surface is dry before use.
- Always pre-heat your crepe maker before using.

- Allow your crepes to cook on the surface (usually around 45-50 secs). Don't be tempted to over cook.
- If not provided with your crepe making device, make sure you have a large heat proof spatula/ food slice to move and turn your crepe.
- Your crepe should be a pale golden colour when cooked. If you find a crepe is too dark in colour reduce the temperature setting.
- If cooking in batches, store your crepes on a warm place with grease proof paper in between to prevent sticking.
- Crepes can be folded, rolled or wrapped around a filing. Try experimenting depending on your choice of topping/filling.
- Remember to switch off your appliance after use.
- Allow to completely cool before cleaning. Use only a damp cloth clean the surface. Do not use any abrasive materials or detergents.
- For any stubborn dried-on foods, brush with a little oil or melted butter, allow to stand for 5 mins then wipe with a damp cloth.

ABOUT COOKNATION

CookNation is the leading publisher of innovative and practical recipe books for the modern cook.

With a range of #1 best-selling titles - from the innovative 'Skinny' calorie-counted series, to the 5:2 Diet Recipes collection and I Love My range - CookNation recipe books have something for everyone.

Visit **www.bellmackenzie.com** to browse the full catalogue.

CREPE FILLINGS

QUICK & EASY NUTELLA CHOCOLATE CREPE

Makes 5 crepes

INGREDIENTS

- 2 free-range eggs
- 200ml/7floz Milk
- 1 tsp sugar
- 125g/4oz plain flour
- ½ tsp butter
- 3 tbsp Nutella chocolate spread

METHOD

1 Preheat the crepe maker whilst you crack the eggs into a bowl and beat with a fork. Stir in the milk and sugar. Sieve the flour into the mixture and whisk well or blend until a smooth lump-free batter is created.

2 Brush the heated crepe plate with butter before pouring on a thin layer of the mixture. Use a T-Stick or spreader to smooth the mixture evenly over the plate. Allow to cook for 60 seconds before gently flipping the crepe to cook the other side. Cook the other side for 60 seconds or until golden.

3 Repeat this cooking method for each crepe. Spread the Nutella across each crepe, covering them whilst leaving approximately a 1cm edge around the crepe uncovered. Either fold or roll the crepe to serve.

CHEFS NOTE

Dust with cocoa powder to serve and add chocolate chips and/or nuts for an extra special treat.

QUICK & EASY PEANUT BUTTER & JELLY CREPE

Makes 5 crepes

INGREDIENTS

- 2 free-range eggs
- 200ml/7floz milk
- 1 tsp sugar
- 125g/4oz plain flour
- ½ tsp butter
- 2 tbsp smooth peanut butter
- 2 tbsp strawberry jam

CHEFS NOTE

Use a crunchy peanut butter if you prefer to add texture to your crepe.

METHOD

1 Preheat the crepe maker whilst you crack the eggs into a bowl and beat with a fork. Stir in the milk and sugar. Sieve the flour into the mixture and whisk well or blend until a smooth lump-free batter is created.

2 Brush the heated crepe plate with butter before pouring on a thin layer of the mixture. Use a T-Stick or spreader to smooth the mixture evenly over the plate. Allow to cook for 60 seconds before gently flipping the crepe to cook the other side. Cook the other side for 60 seconds or until golden.

3 Repeat this cooking method for each crepe. Spread the peanut butter across each crepe, covering them whilst leaving approximately a 1cm edge around the crepe uncovered. Repeat with the strawberry jam, spreading the jam on top of the peanut butter. Either fold or roll the crepe ready to serve.

CARAMELISED APPLE FILLED CREPE

Makes 5 crepes

INGREDIENTS

- 3 cooking apples,
- 2 tbsp caster sugar
- 1 tbsp water
- 2 free-range eggs
- 175ml/6floz milk
- 25ml/1floz water
- 125g/4oz plain flour
- ½ tsp butter

CHEFS NOTE

Stew the apples earlier in the day and store in the fridge to save cooking time.

METHOD

1 Preheat the crepe maker whilst you bring a pan to heat. Peel the apples removing the core and pips and cut into small cubes. Add the apples into the pan along with the water and sugar, cover and leave to cook for 3-5 minutes or until the apples are softening and beginning to dissolve into a mixture. Once caramelised, take the mixture off the heat and place to one side to shortly serve.

2 Crack the eggs into a bowl and beat with a fork. Stir in the milk and water. Sieve the flour into the mixture and whisk well or blend until a smooth lump-free batter is created.

3 Brush the heated crepe plate with butter before pouring on a thin layer of the mixture. Use a T-Stick or spreader to smooth the mixture evenly over the plate. Allow to cook for 60 seconds before gently flipping the crepe to cook the other side. Cook the other side for 60 seconds or until golden.

4 Repeat this cooking method for each crepe. Spread the caramelised apple mixture across each crepe, covering them whilst leaving approximately a 1cm edge around the crepe uncovered. Either fold or roll the crepe to serve.

SUPER STRAWBERRY & CREAM FILLED CREPE

Makes 5 crepes

INGREDIENTS

- 2 free-range eggs
- 175ml/6floz milk
- 25ml/1floz water
- 1 tsp caster sugar
- 125g/4oz plain flour
- ½ tsp butter
- 250g/9oz Strawberries
- Freshly Whipped Cream

CHEFS NOTE

Finely chop fresh mint leaves to add a delicious summer freshness to this recipe.

METHOD

1 Preheat the crepe maker whilst you crack the eggs into a bowl and beat with a fork. Stir in the milk, water and sugar. Sieve the flour into the mixture and whisk well or blend until a smooth lump-free batter is created.

2 Brush the heated crepe plate with butter before pouring on a thin layer of the mixture. Use a T-Stick or spreader to smooth the mixture evenly over the plate. Allow to cook for 60 seconds before gently flipping the crepe to cook the other side. Cook the other side for 60 seconds or until golden.

3 Repeat this cooking method for each crepe. Remove the stalk and leaves from the strawberries and cut them into thin and event slices. Arrange the strawberries in the middle of each crepe, creating a central line of strawberries for almost the full width of the crepe. Cover the strawberries in as little or as much whipped cream as you wish and either fold or roll the crepe ready to eat.

CINNAMON & TOFFEE APPLE FILLED CREPE

Makes 5 crepes

INGREDIENTS

- 3 cooking apples
- 2 tbsp brown sugar
- 1 tsp ground cinnamon
- 1 tbsp water
- 2 free-range eggs
- 175ml/6floz milk
- 25ml/1floz water
- 125g/4oz plain flour
- ½ tsp Butter
- Toffee Sauce for serving

METHOD

1 Preheat the crepe maker whilst you bring a pan to heat. Peel the apples removing the core and pips and cut into small cubes. Add the apples into the pan along with the water, sugar and cinnamon, cover and leave to cook for 3-5 minutes or until the apples are softening and beginning to dissolve into a mixture. Once caramelised, take the mixture off the heat and place to one side to shortly serve.

2 Crack the eggs into a bowl and beat with a fork. Stir in the milk and water. Sieve the flour into the mixture and whisk well or blend until a smooth lump-free batter is created.

3 Brush the heated crepe plate with butter before pouring on a thin layer of the mixture. Use a T-Stick or spreader to smooth the mixture evenly over the plate. Allow to cook for 60 seconds before gently flipping the crepe to cook the other side. Cook the other side for 60 seconds or until golden.

4 Repeat this cooking method for each crepe. Spread the caramelised cinnamon and apple mixture across each crepe, covering them whilst leaving approximately a 1cm edge around the crepe uncovered. Either fold or roll the crepes to serve and drizzle over the toffee sauce to serve.

CHEFS NOTE

Delicious served with a spoonful of real vanilla ice cream.

TRIPLE CHOCOLATE FILLED CREPE

Makes 5 crepes

INGREDIENTS

- 2 free-range eggs
- 200ml/7floz milk
- 1 tsp sugar
- 125g/4oz plain Flour
- ½ tsp butter
- 75g/3oz milk chocolate chunks
- 50g/2oz white chocolate chunks
- 50g/2oz dark chocolate chunks

CHEFS NOTE

Best served straight from the pan. Add a drizzle of caramel sauce on top if your sweet tooth can handle it.

METHOD

1 Preheat the crepe maker whilst you crack the eggs into a bowl and beat with a fork. Stir in the milk and sugar. Sieve the flour into the mixture and whisk well or blend until a smooth lump-free batter is created.

2 Brush the heated crepe plate with butter before pouring on a thin layer of the mixture. Use a T-Stick or spreader to smooth the mixture evenly over the plate. Allow to cook for 60 seconds before gently flipping the crepe to cook the other side. Cook the other side for 60 seconds or until golden.

3 Repeat this cooking method for each crepe. Sprinkle the mixed chocolate chunks down the middle of each crepe forming a central line that covers almost the entire width of the crepe if you wish to roll the crepe, or sprinkle the chocolate chunks in one quarter of the crepe if you wish to fold into quarters to serve. Once rolled or folded, bring a pan to heat and carefully place the chocolate-filled crepe in the pan, allowing the chocolate to begin to melt. Once much of the chocolate has melted, but before the crepe has cooked much more, remove the crepe from the pan and serve.

FRESH PEACH & HONEY CREPE

Makes 5 crepes

INGREDIENTS

- 2 free-range eggs
- 175ml/6floz milk
- 25ml/1floz water
- 1 tsp sugar
- 125g/4oz plain flour
- ½ tsp butter
- 3 large peaches
- 3 tbsp honey

CHEFS NOTE

Serve with a dollop of freshly whipped cream as a treat.

METHOD

1 Preheat the crepe maker whilst you crack the eggs into a bowl and beat with a fork. Stir in the milk, water and sugar. Sieve the flour into the mixture and whisk well or blend until a smooth lump-free batter is created.

2 Brush the heated crepe plate with butter before pouring on a thin layer of the mixture. Use a T-Stick or spreader to smooth the mixture evenly over the plate. Allow to cook for 60 seconds before gently flipping the crepe to cook the other side. Cook the other side for 60 seconds or until golden.

3 Repeat this cooking method for each crepe. Peel the peaches, removing the core and stone of each, and cut it into thin slices. Lay the slices of peach in each of the crepes, overlapping the slices slightly. Drizzle the honey on top of the peach slices and fold the crepe to serve.

RED BERRY FILLED CREPE

Makes 5 crepes

INGREDIENTS

- 50g/2oz strawberries
- 50g/2oz raspberries
- 75g/3oz redcurrants
- 2 tsp sugar
- 2 free-range eggs
- 175ml/6floz milk
- 25ml/1floz water
- 125g/4oz plain flour
- ½ tsp butter

CHEFS NOTE

For a winter warmer take on this recipe, stew the berries with some Christmas spices for a delicious, warm filling.

METHOD

1 Preheat the crepe maker whilst you prepare the berry filling: place all the berries in a bowl, add the sugar and gently mash until a juicy, textured mixture is created. Place to one side.

2 Crack the eggs into a bowl and beat with a fork. Stir in the milk and water. Sieve the flour into the mixture and whisk well or blend until a smooth lump-free batter is created.

3 Brush the heated crepe plate with butter before pouring on a thin layer of the mixture. Use a T-Stick or spreader to smooth the mixture evenly over the plate. Allow to cook for 60 seconds before gently flipping the crepe to cook the other side. Cook the other side for 60 seconds or until golden.

4 Repeat this cooking method for each crepe. Spread the berry mixture across each crepe and either fold or roll the crepe to serve.

BANANA, BLUEBERRY & BLACKCURRANT CREPE

Makes 5 crepes

INGREDIENTS

- 75g/3oz blueberries
- 75g/3oz blackcurrants
- 2 tsp sugar
- 2 free-range eggs
- 175ml/6floz milk
- 25ml/1floz water
- 125g/4oz plain flour
- ½ tsp butter
- 2 bananas

CHEFS NOTE

For a creamier twist either serve with a spoonful of fresh cream or ice cream on the side

METHOD

1 Preheat the crepe maker whilst you prepare the berry filling: place all the berries in a bowl, add the sugar and gently mash until a juicy, textured mixture is created. Place to one side.

2 Crack the eggs into a bowl and beat with a fork. Stir in the milk and water. Sieve the flour into the mixture and whisk well or blend until a smooth lump-free batter is created.

3 Brush the heated crepe plate with butter before pouring on a thin layer of the mixture. Use a T-Stick or spreader to smooth the mixture evenly over the plate. Allow to cook for 60 seconds before gently flipping the crepe to cook the other side. Cook the other side for 60 seconds or until golden.

4 Repeat this cooking method for each crepe. Spread the berry mixture in one quarter of the crepe. Peel and finely slice the bananas, laying the slices on top of the berry mixture. Fold each crepe into quarters to serve.

RASPBERRY AND DARK CHOCOLATE CREPE

Makes 5 crepes

INGREDIENTS

- 2 free-range eggs
- 175ml/6floz milk
- 25ml/1floz water
- 1 tsp sugar
- 125g/4oz plain flour
- ½ tsp butter
- 3 tbsp fresh cream
- 150g/5oz raspberries
- 3 tbsp grated dark chocolate

CHEFS NOTE

If you are not a dark chocolate fan then try this with grated white chocolate.

METHOD

1 Preheat the crepe maker whilst you crack the eggs into a bowl and beat with a fork. Stir in the milk, water and sugar. Sieve the flour into the mixture and whisk well or blend until a smooth lump-free batter is created.

2 Brush the heated crepe plate with butter before pouring on a thin layer of the mixture. Use a T-Stick or spreader to smooth the mixture evenly over the plate. Allow to cook for 60 seconds before gently flipping the crepe to cook the other side. Cook the other side for 60 seconds or until golden.

3 Repeat this cooking method for each crepe. Lightly spread the cream across each crepe and place the raspberries either in one quarter or third if you wish to fold the crepe or in a line if you wish to roll it to serve. Sprinkle the grated dark chocolate over the raspberries and fold or roll to eat.

MELTED CHOCOLATE & MARSHMALLOW CREPE

Makes 5 crepes

INGREDIENTS

- 1½ tsp butter
- 200g/7oz white chocolate
- 125g/4oz of mini marshmallows
- 2 Eggs
- 200ml/7floz milk
- 1 tsp sugar
- 125g/4oz plain flour

CHEFS NOTE

Add in some raspberries for a deliciously fruity flavour.

METHOD

1 Preheat the crepe maker whilst you bring a pan to heat. Melt 1 tsp butter in the pan and on a low heat melt the white chocolate and marshmallows into a lumpy, gooey mixture. Place to one side ready to serve.

2 Crack the eggs into a bowl and beat with a fork. Stir in the milk and sugar. Sieve the flour into the mixture and whisk well or blend until a smooth lump-free batter is created.

3 Brush the heated crepe plate with butter before pouring on a thin layer of the mixture. Use a T-Stick or spreader to smooth the mixture evenly over the plate. Allow to cook for 60 seconds before gently flipping the crepe to cook the other side. Cook the other side for 60 seconds or until golden.

4 Repeat this cooking method for each crepe. Spread the chocolate and marshmallow mixture across the crepe and either fold or roll the crepe to serve.

FRUIT SALAD CREPE

Makes 5 crepes

INGREDIENTS

- 2 free-range eggs
- 175ml/6floz milk
- 25ml/1floz water
- 1 tsp sugar
- 125g/4oz plain flour
- ½ tsp butter
- 125g/4oz pineapple
- 75g/2oz orange segments
- 100g/3½oz strawberries

METHOD

1 Preheat the crepe maker whilst you crack the eggs into a bowl and beat with a fork. Stir in the milk, water and sugar. Sieve the flour into the mixture and whisk well or blend until a smooth lump-free batter is created.

2 Brush the heated crepe plate with butter before pouring on a thin layer of the mixture. Use a T-Stick or spreader to smooth the mixture evenly over the plate. Allow to cook for 60 seconds before gently flipping the crepe to cook the other side. Cook the other side for 60 seconds or until golden.

3 Repeat this cooking method for each crepe. Prepare the fruit by peeling and cutting the pineapple into fine slices; peeling the orange and cut the segments in half or leave whole if you prefer. Remove the stalk and leaves from the strawberries and cut into fine slices. Place the mixed fruit into one third or quarter of the crepe and fold accordingly to serve.

CHEFS NOTE

Serve with a dollop of freshly whipped cream.

MANGO AND PINEAPPLE CREPE

Makes 5 crepes

INGREDIENTS

- 2 free-range eggs
- 175ml/6floz milk
- 25ml/1floz water
- 1 tsp sugar
- 125g/4oz plain flour
- ½ tsp butter
- 150g/5oz Mango
- 150g/5oz Pineapple

CHEFS NOTE

To sweeten things up, drizzle honey over the fruit before folding the crepe to serve.

METHOD

1 Preheat the crepe maker whilst you crack the eggs into a bowl and beat with a fork. Stir in the milk, water and sugar. Sieve the flour into the mixture and whisk well or blend until a smooth lump-free batter is created.

2 Brush the heated crepe plate with butter before pouring on a thin layer of the mixture. Use a T-Stick or spreader to smooth the mixture evenly over the plate. Allow to cook for 60 seconds before gently flipping the crepe to cook the other side. Cook the other side for 60 seconds or until golden.

3 Repeat this cooking method for each crepe. Prepare the fruit by peeling the mango, removing the core and cutting into very small cubes. Peel the pineapple and cut in the same way. Mix both fruits together and place into one quarter of the crepe and fold to serve.

ROCKY ROAD FILLED CREPE

Makes 5 crepes

INGREDIENTS

- 25g/1oz Chocolate Chips
- 25g/1oz Mini Marshmallows
- 2 Eggs
- 200ml / 7fl oz Milk
- ½ tsp Caster Sugar
- ½ tsp Cocoa Powder
- 125g / 4oz Plain Flour
- ½ tsp Butter
- 1 Digestive Biscuit
- 2 tbsp Chocolate Sauce

METHOD

1 Preheat the crepe maker whilst you place a pan on a low heat. Place the chocolate chips and mini marshmallows in the pan and begin to gently melt. Once melting but not over-cooking, remove from the heat and place to one side.

2 Crack the eggs into a bowl and beat with a fork. Stir in the milk, water, sugar and cocoa powder. Sieve the flour into the mixture and whisk well or blend until a smooth lump-free batter is created.

3 Brush the heated crepe plate with butter before pouring on a thin layer of the mixture. Use a T-Stick or spreader to smooth the mixture evenly over the plate. Allow to cook for 60 seconds before gently flipping the crepe to cook the other side. Cook the other side for 60 seconds or until golden.

4 Repeat this cooking method for each crepe. Spoon the chocolate and marshmallow mixture onto each crepe. Crush and crumble the digestive biscuit on top and fold to serve. Finish off by drizzling the chocolate sauce over the crepe and enjoy.

CHEFS NOTE

Best served warm - place the rolled crepe in the pan to heat through before serving & drizzling the sauce.

COCONUT CREAM CREPE

Makes 5 crepes

INGREDIENTS

- 2 free-range eggs
- 175ml/6floz milk
- 25ml/1floz water
- 1 tsp sugar
- 125g/4oz plain flour
- ½ tsp butter
- 200g/7oz fresh coconut
- 3 tbsp freshly whipped cream
- 2 tbsp coconut flakes

METHOD

1 Preheat the crepe maker whilst you crack the eggs into a bowl and beat with a fork. Stir in the milk, water and sugar. Sieve the flour into the mixture and whisk well or blend until a smooth lump-free batter is created.

2 Brush the heated crepe plate with butter before pouring on a thin layer of the mixture. Use a T-Stick or spreader to smooth the mixture evenly over the plate. Allow to cook for 60 seconds before gently flipping the crepe to cook the other side. Cook the other side for 60 seconds or until golden.

3 Repeat this cooking method for each crepe. Blend the coconut, cream and flakes in a food processor to make a smooth cream. Spread the cream over each crepe and roll or fold to serve.

CHEFS NOTE

For a sweeter treat, add some milk chocolate chunks into the crepe.

CHOCOLATE, HAZELNUT & STRAWBERRY CREPE

Makes 5 crepes

INGREDIENTS

- 3 tsp butter
- 125g/4oz milk chocolate chunks
- 25g/1oz hazelnuts, crushed
- 2 free-range eggs
- 175ml/6floz milk
- 25ml/1floz water
- 1 tsp sugar
- 125g/4oz Plain Flour
- 150g/5oz Strawberries

METHOD

1 Preheat the crepe maker whilst you bring a pan to heat. Melt 2 tsp of the butter and begin to melt the chocolate. Stir in the crushed hazelnuts and place the mixture to one side before it over cooks.

2 Crack the eggs into a bowl and beat with a fork. Stir in the milk, water and sugar. Sieve the flour into the mixture and whisk well or blend until a smooth lump-free batter is created.

3 Brush the heated crepe plate with the remaining butter before pouring on a thin layer of the mixture. Use a T-Stick or spreader to smooth the mixture evenly over the plate. Allow to cook for 60 seconds before gently flipping the crepe to cook the other side. Cook the other side for 60 seconds or until golden.

4 Repeat this cooking method for each crepe. Spread the chocolate and hazelnut mixture onto each crepe. Remove the stalks and leaves from the strawberries and finely slice. Lay the slices on top of the chocolate and hazelnut mixture and fold or roll the crepe to serve.

CHEFS NOTE

As a healthier alternative, use dark cocoa chocolate rather than milk.

VANILLA AND WHITE CHOCOLATE CREPE

Makes 5 crepes

INGREDIENTS

- 3 tsp butter
- 125g/4oz white chocolate chunks
- 4 tbsp single cream
- 2 tsp caster sugar
- 1 tsp vanilla extract
- 2 free-range eggs
- 175ml/6floz milk
- 25ml/1floz water
- 125g/4oz plain flour

METHOD

1 Preheat the crepe maker whilst you bring a pan to heat. Melt the 2 tsp of the butter and begin to melt the chocolate. Stir in the cream, sugar and vanilla extract and place the mixture to one side before it over cooks.

2 Crack the eggs into a bowl and beat with a fork. Stir in the milk and water. Sieve the flour into the mixture and whisk well or blend until a smooth lump-free batter is created.

3 Brush the heated crepe plate with the remaining butter before pouring on a thin layer of the mixture. Use a T-Stick or spreader to smooth the mixture evenly over the plate. Allow to cook for 60 seconds before gently flipping the crepe to cook the other side. Cook the other side for 60 seconds or until golden.

4 Repeat this cooking method for each crepe. Spread the white chocolate mixture thinly across each crepe. Fold or roll the crepe to serve.

CHEFS NOTE

Best served warm! Serve with a scoop of vanilla ice cream to provide a cool contrast.

CARAMELISED RED ONION CREPE

Makes 5 crepes

INGREDIENTS

- 1 tbsp olive oil
- 2 red onion, finely chopped
- 2 tbsp balsamic vinegar
- 1 tbsp brown sugar
- 2 free-range eggs
- 175ml/6floz milk
- 25ml/1floz water
- Pinch of salt
- Pinch of pepper
- 125g/4oz plain flour
- ½ tsp butter

CHEFS NOTE

Try serving with a drizzle of honey too.

METHOD

1 Preheat the crepe maker whilst you bring a pan to heat. Drizzle the olive oil to heat in the pan and finely chop the onion. Add the onions into the pan and cook on a medium heat for 3-5 minutes or until the onions are beginning to soften and turn golden brown. Add the balsamic vinegar and sugar and sauté for a further 1-2 minutes or until the sugar has dissolved. Remove from the heat and place to one side.

2 Crack the eggs into a bowl and beat with a fork. Stir in the milk and water, along with the salt and pepper. Sieve the flour into the mixture and whisk well or blend until a smooth lump-free batter is created.

3 Brush the heated crepe plate with butter before pouring on a thin layer of the mixture. Use a T-Stick or spreader to smooth the mixture evenly over the plate. Allow to cook for 60 seconds before gently flipping the crepe to cook the other side. Cook the other side for 60 seconds or until golden.

4 Repeat this cooking method for each crepe. Spoon the caramelised onion mixture across the crepes, fold or roll the crepe to serve.

SMOKED SALMON AND AVOCADO CREPE

Makes 5 crepes

INGREDIENTS

- 2 free-range eggs
- 175ml/6floz milk
- 25ml/1floz water
- Pinch of salt
- Pinch of pepper
- 125g/4oz plain flour
- ½ tsp Butter
- 4 tbsp Cream Cheese
- 250g/9oz Smoked Salmon
- 2 avocados

METHOD

1 Preheat the crepe maker whilst you crack the eggs into a bowl and beat with a fork. Stir in the milk and water, along with the salt and pepper. Sieve the flour into the mixture and whisk well or blend until a smooth lump-free batter is created.

2 Brush the heated crepe plate with butter before pouring on a thin layer of the mixture. Use a T-Stick or spreader to smooth the mixture evenly over the plate. Allow to cook for 60 seconds before gently flipping the crepe to cook the other side. Cook the other side for 60 seconds or until golden.

3 Repeat this cooking method for each crepe. Spread the cream cheese lightly across each crepe and top with torn pieces of the smoked salmon. Slice the avocado and layer the pieces over the salmon and cream cheese. Fold or roll the crepe to serve.

CHEFS NOTE

Use perfectly ripe avocados for the best flavour.

ASPARAGUS & PANCETTA FILLED CREPE

Makes 5 crepes

INGREDIENTS

- 2 bunches thin stalks of asparagus
- 2 tbsp olive oil
- 150g/5oz pancetta
- 2 free-range eggs
- 175ml/6floz milk
- 25ml/1floz water
- Pinch of salt
- Pinch of pepper
- 125g/4oz plain flour
- ½ tsp butter
- 3 tbsp cream cheese

CHEFS NOTE

Instead of using cream cheese, try sprinkling some finely grated Parmesan on top of the pancetta.

METHOD

1 Preheat the crepe maker and bring a pan to boil. Either boil or steam the asparagus for a few minutes until the stalks are tender. Bring a pan to heat, add in the olive oil, and fry the pancetta for 4 – 5 minutes or until cooked through. Cook for longer if you prefer them a little crispier.

2 Crack the eggs into a bowl and beat with a fork. Stir in the milk and water, along with the salt and pepper. Sieve the flour into the mixture and whisk well or blend until a smooth lump-free batter is created.

3 Brush the heated crepe plate with butter before pouring on a thin layer of the mixture. Use a T-Stick or spreader to smooth the mixture evenly over the plate. Allow to cook for 60 seconds before gently flipping the crepe to cook the other side. Cook the other side for 60 seconds or until golden.

4 Repeat this cooking method for each crepe. Spread the cream cheese lightly across each crepe and place 2 thick or 3 thin asparagus on each wrap, slightly off centre. Add the pancetta, drizzling in some of the oils from the pan as well for flavour. Gently roll the crepe ready to serve.

CARROT CREPE

Makes 5 crepes

INGREDIENTS

- 2 free-range eggs
- 175ml/6floz milk
- 25ml/1floz water
- Pinch of salt
- Pinch of pepper
- 2 carrots
- 125g/4oz plain flour
- ½ tsp butter
- 5 tbsp cream cheese
- Freshly chopped Chives to serve

CHEFS NOTE

Add a teaspoon of mixed spice to give this a winter warming kick.

METHOD

1 Preheat the crepe maker whilst you crack the eggs into a bowl and beat with a fork. Stir in the milk and water, along with the salt and pepper. Peel the carrot and finely grate into the mixture. Sieve the flour into the mixture and whisk well or blend until a smooth lump-free batter is created.

2 Brush the heated crepe plate with butter before pouring on a thin layer of the mixture. Use a T-Stick or spreader to smooth the mixture evenly over the plate. Allow to cook for 60 seconds before gently flipping the crepe to cook the other side. Cook the other side for 60 seconds or until golden.

3 Repeat this cooking method for each crepe. Fold each crepe into quarters and serve with a spoonful of cream cheese. Sprinkle the freshly chopped chives on top and enjoy.

LOADED HAM AND CHEESE CREPE

Makes 5 crepes

INGREDIENTS

- 2 free-range eggs
- 200ml/7floz milk
- Pinch of salt
- Pinch of pepper
- 2 small carrots
- 125g/4oz plain flour
- ½ tsp Butter
- 5 slices of honey roast ham
- 200g/7oz grated Cheddar Cheese

CHEFS NOTE

Best served hot, straight from the pan! Try swapping Cheddar with Red Leicester for a stronger flavour.

METHOD

1 Preheat the crepe maker whilst you crack the eggs into a bowl and beat with a fork. Stir in the milk and water, along with the salt and pepper. Sieve the flour into the mixture and whisk well or blend until a smooth lump-free batter is created.

2 Brush the heated crepe plate with butter before pouring on a thin layer of the mixture. Use a T-Stick or spreader to smooth the mixture evenly over the plate. Allow to cook for 60 seconds before gently flipping the crepe to cook the other side. Cook the other side for 60 seconds or until golden.

3 Repeat this cooking method for each crepe. Tear the ham into smaller pieces and place on top of each crepe along with some grated cheese. Roll or fold the crepe and place in the pan to melt the cheese slightly. Be careful not to overcook the crepe itself. Remove from the pan and serve.

LIGHT PARMA HAM CREPE

Makes 5 crepes

INGREDIENTS

- 2 free-range eggs
- 200ml /7fl oz milk
- Pinch of salt
- Pinch of pepper
- 125g/4oz plain flour
- ½ tsp butter
- 3 tbsp cream cheese
- 10 slices of Parma Ham
- Freshly chopped Chives to serve

METHOD

1 Preheat the crepe maker whilst you crack the eggs into a bowl and beat with a fork. Stir in the milk and the salt and pepper. Sieve the flour into the mixture and whisk well or blend until a smooth lump-free batter is created.

2 Brush the heated crepe plate with butter before pouring on a thin layer of the mixture. Use a T-Stick or spreader to smooth the mixture evenly over the plate. Allow to cook for 60 seconds before gently flipping the crepe to cook the other side. Cook the other side for 60 seconds or until golden.

3 Repeat this cooking method for each crepe. Lightly spread the cream cheese across each crepe and lay 2 slices of Parma Ham in one quarter of each crepe. Fold each crepe into quarters and serve with a sprinkling of freshly chopped chives.

CHEFS NOTE

This works just as well with bresola in place of the Parma ham.

RED PESTO AND PANCETTA CREPE

Makes 5 crepes

INGREDIENTS

- 150g/5oz pancetta
- 2 free-range eggs
- 200ml/7floz milk
- Pinch of salt
- Pinch of pepper
- 2 tbsp Red Pesto
- 125g/4oz Plain Flour
- ½ tsp butter
- Fresh Rocket Leaves to serve

CHEFS NOTE

A sprinkling of finely grated cheese on top can make a wonderful addition to this recipe.

METHOD

1 Preheat the crepe maker whilst you bring a pan to heat. Fry the pancetta for 4-5 minutes until it is cooked through. Cook for slightly longer if you prefer yours crispy.

2 Crack the eggs into a bowl and beat with a fork. Stir in the milk, the salt and pepper and the red pesto. Sieve the flour into the mixture and whisk well or blend until a smooth lump-free batter is created.

3 Brush the heated crepe plate with butter before pouring on a thin layer of the mixture. Use a T-Stick or spreader to smooth the mixture evenly over the plate. Allow to cook for 60 seconds before gently flipping the crepe to cook the other side. Cook the other side for 60 seconds or until golden.

4 Repeat this cooking method for each crepe. Spoon the cooked pancetta onto each crepe, allowing some oils from the pan to drizzle on too for flavour. Fold or roll each crepe to serve.

GARLIC AND SPINACH CREPE

Makes 5 crepes

INGREDIENTS

- 2 large handfuls of spinach leaves
- 1 tbsp olive oil
- 2 clove of garlic, crushed
- 2 free-range eggs
- 175ml/6floz milk
- 25ml/1floz water
- Pinch of salt
- Pinch of pepper
- 125g/4oz plain flour
- ½ tsp butter

CHEFS NOTE

Add some finely grated Parmesan either on top of the garlic spinach or on top of the crepe for extra flavour.

METHOD

1 Preheat the crepe maker whilst you warm a pan with the olive oil and garlic. Add the spinach leaves into the pan and cook for a few minutes until the leaves begin to soften and wilt.

2 Crack the eggs into a bowl and beat with a fork. Stir in the milk and water along with the salt and pepper. Sieve the flour into the mixture and whisk well or blend until a smooth lump-free batter is created.

3 Brush the heated crepe plate with butter before pouring on a thin layer of the mixture. Use a T-Stick or spreader to smooth the mixture evenly over the plate. Allow to cook for 60 seconds before gently flipping the crepe to cook the other side. Cook the other side for 60 seconds or until golden.

4 Repeat this cooking method for each crepe. Spoon the garlic spinach on top of each crepe and fold or roll to serve.

SPINACH AND RICOTTA FILLED CREPE

Makes 5 crepes

INGREDIENTS

- 3 large handfuls of spinach leaves
- 1 tbsp olive oil
- 2 free-range eggs
- 175ml/6floz milk
- 25ml/1floz water
- Pinch of salt
- Pinch of pepper
- 125g/4oz plain flour
- ½ tsp butter
- 5 tbsp ricotta cheese
- 75g/3oz cherry tomatoes

CHEFS NOTE

Swap the cherry tomatoes for button mushrooms for a more savoury option.

METHOD

1 Preheat the crepe maker whilst you warm a pan with the olive oil. Add the spinach leaves into the pan and cook for a few minutes until the leaves begin to soften and wilt.

2 Crack the eggs into a bowl and beat with a fork. Stir in the milk and water along with the salt and pepper. Sieve the flour into the mixture and whisk well or blend until a smooth lump-free batter is created.

3 Brush the heated crepe plate with butter before pouring on a thin layer of the mixture. Use a T-Stick or spreader to smooth the mixture evenly over the plate. Allow to cook for 60 seconds before gently flipping the crepe to cook the other side. Cook the other side for 60 seconds or until golden.

4 Repeat this cooking method for each crepe. Spoon the cooked spinach onto each crepe, adding as much or as little Ricotta as you prefer. Fold or roll the crepes to serve. Slice the tomatoes into halves and serve with the crepes.

MUSHROOM AND LEEK FILLED CREPE

Makes 5 crepes

INGREDIENTS

- 1 tbsp olive oil
- 150g/5oz button mushrooms
- 2 leeks
- 2 free-range eggs
- 175ml/6floz milk
- 25ml/1floz water
- Pinch of salt
- Pinch of pepper
- 125g/4oz plain flour
- ½ tsp butter

CHEFS NOTE

Add 1 tbsp of single cream into the mushroom and leek mixture for a creamier filling

METHOD

1 Preheat the crepe maker whilst you bring a pan to heat. Drizzle in the olive oil and finely chop the button mushrooms and leeks. Add the mushrooms and leeks to the pan and sauté for 4-5 minutes or until they are softening and golden brown. Remove from the heat and place the mixture to one side.

2 Crack the eggs into a bowl and beat with a fork. Stir in the milk and water along with the salt and pepper. Sieve the flour into the mixture and whisk well or blend until a smooth lump-free batter is created.

3 Brush the heated crepe plate with butter before pouring on a thin layer of the mixture. Use a T-Stick or spreader to smooth the mixture evenly over the plate. Allow to cook for 60 seconds before gently flipping the crepe to cook the other side. Cook the other side for 60 seconds or until golden.

4 Repeat this cooking method for each crepe. Spoon the mushroom and leek mixture onto each crepe and fold or roll to serve.

EXTRA CHEESY CREPE

Makes 5 crepes

INGREDIENTS

- 2 free-range eggs
- 200ml/7fl oz milk
- Pinch of salt
- Pinch of pepper
- 125g / 4oz Plain Flour
- ½tsp butter
- 75g /3oz Cheddar Cheese, grated
- 75g /3oz Gruyere Cheese, grated
- 75g /3oz Parmesan Cheese, grated
- Handful of chopped chives

METHOD

1 Preheat the crepe maker whilst you crack the eggs into a bowl and beat with a fork. Stir in the milk and the salt and pepper. Sieve the flour into the mixture and whisk well or blend until a smooth lump-free batter is created.

2 Brush the heated crepe plate with butter before pouring on a thin layer of the mixture. Use a T-Stick or spreader to smooth the mixture evenly over the plate. Allow to cook for 60 seconds before gently flipping the crepe to cook the other side. Cook the other side for 60 seconds or until golden.

3 Repeat this cooking method for each crepe. Bring a pan to heat. Mix the grated cheeses and sprinkle onto each crepe. Roll each crepe and gently place in the pan on a low heat to continue to melt the cheese. Be careful not to overcook the crepe itself. Remove from the pan and serve with chopped chives.

CHEFS NOTE

Add a dash of Worcestershire sauce for an extra kick to your cheesy crepe.

CHEESE AND ONION CREPE

Makes 5 crepes

INGREDIENTS

- 1 tbsp olive oil
- 2 onions, finely sliced
- 2 free-range eggs
- 200ml/7floz milk
- Pinch of salt
- Pinch of pepper
- 125g/4oz plain flour
- ½ tsp butter
- 50g/2oz Cheddar Cheese, grated
- 50g/2oz Gruyere Cheese, grated

CHEFS NOTE

Serve with fresh salad leaves for a healthy accompaniment.

METHOD

1 Preheat the crepe maker whilst you bring a pan to heat. Drizzle in the olive oil, adding in the finely sliced onion. Sauté for 4-5 minutes or until the onions are soft and golden brown.

2 Crack the eggs into a bowl and beat with a fork. Stir in the milk and the salt and pepper. Sieve the flour into the mixture and whisk well or blend until a smooth lump-free batter is created.

3 Brush the heated crepe plate with butter before pouring on a thin layer of the mixture. Use a T-Stick or spreader to smooth the mixture evenly over the plate. Allow to cook for 60 seconds before gently flipping the crepe to cook the other side. Cook the other side for 60 seconds or until golden.

4 Repeat this cooking method for each crepe. Bring a pan to heat. Spoon the sautéed onions on top of each crepe. Sprinkle the mixed grated cheeses on top of the warm onions and allow the cheese to melt. Roll each crepe and gently place in the pan on a low heat to continue to melt the cheese. Be careful not to overcook the crepe itself. Remove from the pan and serve.

CREPE TOPPINGS

TRADITIONAL SWEET CREPE

Makes 5 crepes

INGREDIENTS

- 2 free-range eggs
- 175ml/6floz milk
- 25ml/1floz water
- 125g/4oz plain flour
- ½ tsp butter
- Lemon wedges and sugar for serving

METHOD

1 Preheat the crepe maker whilst you crack the eggs into a bowl and beat with a fork. Stir in the milk and water. Sieve the flour into the mixture and whisk well or blend until a smooth lump-free batter is created.

2 Brush the heated crepe plate with butter before pouring on a thin layer of the mixture. Use a T-Stick or spreader to smooth the mixture evenly over the plate. Allow to cook for 60 seconds before gently flipping the crepe to cook the other side. Cook the other side for 60 seconds or until golden.

3 Repeat this cooking method for each crepe. Drizzle with freshly squeezed lemon juice and sugar.

CHEFS NOTE

For a savoury crepe, add a pinch of salt and pepper.

SUMMER STRAWBERRIES AND CREAM CREPE

Makes 5 crepes

INGREDIENTS

- 2 free-range eggs
- 175ml/6floz milk
- 25ml/1floz water
- ½ tsp caster sugar
- 125g/4oz plain flour
- ½ tsp butter
- 250g/9oz strawberries, sliced
- 6 tbsp fresh cream

METHOD

1 Preheat the crepe maker whilst you crack the eggs into a bowl and beat with a fork. Stir in the milk, water and sugar. Sieve the flour into the mixture and whisk well or blend until a smooth lump-free batter is created.

2 Brush the heated crepe plate with butter before pouring on a thin layer of the mixture. Use a T-Stick or spreader to smooth the mixture evenly over the plate. Allow to cook for 60 seconds before gently flipping the crepe to cook the other side. Cook the other side for 60 seconds or until golden.

3 Repeat this cooking method for each crepe. Cut the fresh strawberries into quarters to serve on top of the crepe along with a dollop of cream.

CHEFS NOTE

Serve with fresh whipped cream for a thicker topping.

BLUEBERRY AND BANANA CREPE

Makes 5 crepes

INGREDIENTS

- 2 free-range eggs
- 200ml/7floz milk
- ½ tbsp caster sugar
- 125g/4oz plain flour
- ½ tsp butter
- 3 bananas, sliced
- 200g/7oz blueberries

METHOD

1 Preheat the crepe maker whilst you crack the eggs into a bowl and beat with a fork. Stir in the milk, water and sugar. Sieve the flour into the mixture and whisk well or blend until a smooth lump-free batter is created.

2 Brush the heated crepe plate with butter before pouring on a thin layer of the mixture. Use a T-Stick or spreader to smooth the mixture evenly over the plate. Allow to cook for 60 seconds before gently flipping the crepe to cook the other side. Cook the other side for 60 seconds or until golden.

3 Repeat this cooking method for each crepe. Slice the bananas and then cut each slice in half. Arrange the banana slices along with the fresh blueberries on top of the crepe ready to serve!

CHEFS NOTE

For a juicier take on this recipe and explosive flavour, pre-stew the blueberries until tender and gently mash them to serve.

CHOCOLATE AND BANANA CREPE

Makes 5 crepes

INGREDIENTS

- 2 free-range eggs
- 200ml/7fl oz milk
- 125g/4oz plain flour
- ½ tsp butter
- 3 bananas, sliced
- 150g/5oz milk chocolate chips
- 5 tsp cocoa powder

CHEFS NOTE

This is just as delicious with white chocolate chunks. You may prefer to swap the cocoa powder for chocolate sauce.

METHOD

1 Preheat the crepe maker whilst you crack the eggs into a bowl and beat with a fork. Stir in the milk and water. Sieve the flour into the mixture and whisk well or blend until a smooth lump-free batter is created.

2 Brush the heated crepe plate with butter before pouring on a thin layer of the mixture. Use a T-Stick or spreader to smooth the mixture evenly over the plate. Allow to cook for 60 seconds before gently flipping the crepe to cook the other side. Cook the other side for 60 seconds or until golden.

3 Repeat this cooking method for each crepe. Slice the bananas and then cut each slice in half ready for serving. Fold the crepes and scatter the milk chocolate chips on top allowing them to melt slightly. Sprinkle over the cocoa powder and top with banana slices to serve.

MIXED SUMMER BERRY CREPE

Makes 5 crepes

INGREDIENTS

- 2 free-range eggs
- 175ml/6floz milk
- 25ml/1floz water
- ½ tbsp caster sugar
- 125g/4oz plain flour
- ½ tsp butter
- 100g/3½oz strawberries
- 125g/4oz raspberries
- 125g/4oz blueberries

METHOD

1 Preheat the crepe maker whilst you crack the eggs into a bowl and beat with a fork. Stir in the milk, water and sugar. Sieve the flour into the mixture and whisk well or blend until a smooth lump-free batter is created.

2 Brush the heated crepe plate with butter before pouring on a thin layer of the mixture. Use a T-Stick or spreader to smooth the mixture evenly over the plate. Allow to cook for 60 seconds before gently flipping the crepe to cook the other side. Cook the other side for 60 seconds or until golden.

3 Repeat this cooking method for each crepe. Cut the fresh strawberries into quarters to serve. Fold the crepe and top with the strawberries, raspberries and blueberries ready to serve.

CHEFS NOTE

A drizzle of cream can make this even more delicious, or a dollop of fruit yoghurt works wonderfully as a healthier alternative.

APPLE CREPE CRUMBLE

Makes 5 crepes

INGREDIENTS

- 3 large cooking apples, peeled & cubed
- 2 free-range eggs
- 175ml/6floz milk
- 25ml/1floz water
- 2 tbsp caster sugar
- 125g/4oz plain flour
- ½ tsp butter
- 200g/7oz crumble mix

METHOD

1 Preheat the crepe maker and bring a small pan of water to boil, whilst you peel the cooking apples. Cut the apples into small cubes, disposing of the core and pips. Stew the apple for 10 minutes or until the apple is soft. Drain and place into a small bowl. Add 1 tbsp sugar and gentle mash the mixture.

2 Crack the eggs into a bowl and beat with a fork. Stir in the milk, water and 1 tbsp sugar. Sieve the flour into the mixture and whisk well or blend until a smooth lump-free batter is created.

3 Brush the heated crepe plate with butter before pouring on a thin layer of the mixture. Use a T-Stick or spreader to smooth the mixture evenly over the plate. Allow to cook for 60 seconds before gently flipping the crepe to cook the other side. Cook the other side for 60 seconds or until golden.

4 Repeat this cooking method for each crepe. Fold the crepe on a plate to serve, spoon the apple on top and sprinkle the crumble mix ready to serve.

CHEFS NOTE

A dash of cinnamon along with a spoonful of vanilla ice cream makes a perfect serving option.

CREPE SUZETTE

Makes 5 crepes

INGREDIENTS

- 1 orange
- 1 lemon
- 200ml/7floz fresh orange juice
- 1 tbsp caster sugar
- 120ml/4floz Grand Marnier
- 2 free-range eggs
- 125g/4oz plain flour
- 175ml/6floz milk
- 25ml/1floz water
- 40g/1½oz butter

CHEFS NOTE

To achieve the traditional crepe suzette flame, once the crepes have been soaked and served, bring the pan off the heat and add a little extra dash of Grand Marnier. Carefully set alight with a flame and pour the flaming sauce over your crepes and voila!

METHOD

1 Preheat the crepe maker while you prepare the sauce: grate the zest of the orange and the lemon into a bowl, stirring in the fresh orange juice, ½ tbsp caster sugar and the Grand Marnier and place to one side.

2 Crack the eggs into a bowl and beat with a fork. Stir in the milk, water and ½ tbsp sugar. Sieve the flour into the mixture and whisk well or blend until a smooth lump-free batter is created.

3 Heat a small pan to warm the sauce and melt the butter. Pour in the sauce mixture and heat through. Brush the heated crepe plate with a dash of butter as well before pouring on a thin layer of the mixture. Use a T-Stick or spreader to smooth the mixture evenly over the plate. Allow to cook for 60 seconds before gently flipping the crepe to cook the other side. Cook the other side for 60 seconds or until golden. Once cooked, place the cooked crepe in the pan with the sauce and allow to soak and warm through.

4 Repeat this cooking method for each crepe. Fold the crepe(s) on a plate to serve, spooning as much or as little of the sauce on top as you wish.

LEMON AND RASPBERRY CREPE

Makes 5 crepes

INGREDIENTS

- 2 free-range eggs
- 200ml/7floz milk
- ½ tsp caster sugar
- 125g/4oz plain flour
- 1 lemon
- ½ tsp butter
- 250g/5oz raspberries
- 1 tsp icing sugar

CHEFS NOTE

For a fresh summer kick, instead of including lemon juice in the crepe itself, just serve with lemon ice cream.

METHOD

1 Preheat the crepe maker whilst you crack the eggs into a bowl and beat with a fork. Stir in the milk, water and sugar. Sieve the flour into the mixture and whisk well or blend until a smooth lump-free batter is created. Squeeze in the juice from the lemon and stir.

2 Grate the zest from the lemon and place to one side ready to serve with the finished crepe. Place most of the raspberries in a small bowl and gently mash with a fork before adding in the remaining raspberries and icing sugar. Again, place to one side ready to serve with the finished crepe.

3 Brush the heated crepe plate with butter before pouring on a thin layer of the mixture. Use a T-Stick or spreader to smooth the mixture evenly over the plate. Allow to cook for 60 seconds before gently flipping the crepe to cook the other side. Cook the other side for 60 seconds or until golden.

4 Repeat this cooking method for each crepe. Fold the crepe in to quarters ready to serve. Spoon the whole and mashed raspberries on top of the crepes and sprinkle over the lemon zest for added flavour.

PEACH AND BRANDY CREPE

Makes 5 crepes

INGREDIENTS

- 5 peaches
- 1 tbsp caster sugar
- 125ml/4floz brandy
- 2 free-range eggs
- 125g/4oz plain flour
- 200ml/7floz milk
- ½ tsp butter
- Freshly whipped cream for serving

METHOD

1 Preheat the crepe maker and bring a small pan of water to boil whilst you peel the peaches. Slice the peaches and discard the stone. Stew the peaches for 10 minutes or until soft. Drain the peaches and place back into the pan but bring off the heat. Lightly mash with a fork, adding the sugar and the brandy. Stir well and place to one side.

2 Crack the eggs into a bowl and beat with a fork. Stir in the milk, water and ½ tbsp sugar. Sieve the flour into the mixture and whisk well or blend until a smooth lump-free batter is created.

3 Brush the heated crepe plate with butter whilst you bring the pan with the peach and brandy mixture back onto a low heat to warm through ready for serving. Pour on to the crepe plate a thin layer of the crepe mixture. Use a T-Stick or spreader to smooth the mixture evenly over the plate. Allow to cook for 60 seconds before gently flipping the crepe to cook the other side. Cook the other side for 60 seconds or until golden.

4 Repeat this cooking method for each crepe. Fold the crepes on a plate, spooning the warmed peach and brandy mixture on top of the crepes. Add a spoonful of freshly whipped cream ready to serve.

CHEFS NOTE

Try swapping the peaches with pears for a winter warmer!

WHITE CHOCOLATE AND BAILEYS CREAM CREPE

Makes 5 crepes

INGREDIENTS

- 700ml/7floz single cream
- 125ml/4floz Baileys
- 1 tbsp caster sugar
- 2 free-range eggs
- 125g/4oz plain flour
- 200ml /7floz milk
- ½ tsp butter
- 200g/7oz white chocolate chips

METHOD

1 Preheat the crepe maker whilst you prepare the baileys cream: mix the single cream, baileys and sugar into a bowl. Whisk hard by hand or an electric whisk to thicken the mixture. Place to one side ready for serving.

2 Crack the eggs into a bowl and beat with a fork. Stir in the milk and water. Sieve the flour into the mixture and whisk well or blend until a smooth lump-free batter is created.

3 Brush the heated crepe plate with butter before pouring on a thin layer of the mixture. Use a T-Stick or spreader to smooth the mixture evenly over the plate. Allow to cook for 60 seconds before gently flipping the crepe to cook the other side. Cook the other side for 60 seconds or until golden.

4 Repeat this cooking method for each crepe. Fold the crepes into quarters, sprinkling on the white chocolate chips or chunks whilst the crepes are still warm to allow the chocolate to melt slightly. Drizzle over the baileys cream and serve.

CHEFS NOTE

Save yourself time by preparing the baileys cream earlier in the day and place in the fridge to keep cool.

HONEY AND NUTMEG CREPE

Makes 5 crepes

INGREDIENTS

- 2 free-range eggs
- 175ml/6floz milk
- 25ml/1floz water
- 1 tsp caster sugar
- 1 tsp ground nutmeg
- 125g/4oz plain flour
- ½ tsp butter
- 200g/7oz hazelnuts, crushed
- Honey for serving

METHOD

1 Preheat the crepe maker whilst you crack the eggs into a bowl and beat with a fork. Stir in the milk, water, sugar and nutmeg. Sieve the flour into the mixture and whisk well or blend until a smooth lump-free batter is created.

2 Brush the heated crepe plate with butter before pouring on a thin layer of the mixture. Use a T-Stick or spreader to smooth the mixture evenly over the plate. Allow to cook for 60 seconds before gently flipping the crepe to cook the other side. Cook the other side for 60 seconds or until golden.

3 Repeat this cooking method for each crepe. Fold the crepes into quarters and sprinkle over the crushed Hazelnuts. Drizzle on top as much or as little honey are you desire and serve.

CHEFS NOTE

Best served warm, straight from the crepe plate. As a little something sweeter, add a dollop of ice cream to serve.

FRUIT SALAD CREPE

Makes 5 crepes

INGREDIENTS

- 200g/7oz strawberries
- 1 tbsp caster sugar
- 2 free-range eggs
- 125g/4oz plain flour
- 200ml/7floz milk
- ½ tsp butter
- 3 kiwis, sliced
- 3 bananas, sliced

CHEFS NOTE

Try swapping the strawberries with blueberries or blackberries if you like.

METHOD

1 Preheat the crepe maker and a small pan. Pick or cut the stalk and leaves off the strawberries and cut them into quarters and place in the pan. Stir the strawberries and mash them as they cook to create a coulis. Add ½ tbsp sugar and stir well. Once a lumpy, liquid mixture, place to one side ready to serve.

2 Crack the eggs into a bowl and beat with a fork. Stir in the milk and water. Sieve the flour into the mixture and whisk well or blend until a smooth lump-free batter is created.

3 Brush the heated crepe plate with butter before pouring on a thin layer of the mixture. Use a T-Stick or spreader a T-Stick or spreader to smooth the mixture evenly over the plate. Allow to cook for 60 seconds before gently flipping the crepe to cook the other side. Cook the other side for 60 seconds or until golden.

4 Repeat this cooking method for each crepe. Peel and slice the kiwis & bananas and serve on top of the crepes. Drizzle over the strawberry coulis and serve.

CHOCOLATE BERRY CREPE

Makes 5 crepes

INGREDIENTS

- 2 free-range eggs
- 125g/4oz plain flour
- 200ml/7floz milk
- ½ tsp caster sugar
- 2 tbsp cocoa powder
- ½ tsp butter
- 3 tbsp Nutella chocolate spread
- 150g/5oz strawberries, sliced
- 150g/5oz raspberries

CHEFS NOTE

For a delightful dessert treat, serve in an ice cream glass topped with a scoop of your favourite ice cream.

METHOD

1 Preheat the crepe maker whilst you crack the eggs into a bowl and beat with a fork. Stir in the milk, sugar and cocoa powder. Sieve the flour into the mixture and whisk well or blend until a smooth lump-free batter is created.

2 Brush the heated crepe plate with butter before pouring on a thin layer of the mixture. Use a T-Stick or spreader to smooth the mixture evenly over the plate. Allow to cook for 60 seconds before gently flipping the crepe to cook the other side. Cook the other side for 60 seconds or until golden.

3 Repeat this cooking method for each crepe. Fold the crepes into quarters to serve. Spread the Nutella Chocolate over the crepe. Cut the fresh strawberries into quarters and, along with the whole raspberries, serve on top of the Nutella and enjoy!

VANILLA FUDGE CREPE

Makes 5 crepes

INGREDIENTS

- 2 free-range eggs
- 200ml/7floz milk
- 1 tsp caster sugar
- 1 tsp vanilla extract
- 125g/4oz plain flour
- ½ tsp butter
- 200g/7oz fudge, cubed
- 5 tbsp hot fudge sauce
- 5 scoops vanilla ice cream

METHOD

1 Preheat the crepe maker whilst you crack the eggs into a bowl and beat with a fork. Stir in the milk, sugar and vanilla essence. Sieve the flour into the mixture and whisk well or blend until a smooth lump-free batter is created.

2 Brush the heated crepe plate with butter before pouring on a thin layer of the mixture. Use a T-Stick or spreader to smooth the mixture evenly over the plate. Allow to cook for 60 seconds before gently flipping the crepe to cook the other side. Cook the other side for 60 seconds or until golden.

3 Repeat this cooking method for each crepe. Fold the crepes into quarters to serve. Cut the fudge into small cubes and scatter over the crepes, drizzling on top the hot fudge sauce. Serve with a scoop (or two!) of vanilla ice cream.

CHEFS NOTE

If serving for friends, add vanilla seeds or beans for an impressive twist.

ROCKY ROAD CREPE

Makes 5 crepes

INGREDIENTS

- 2 free-range eggs
- 200ml/7floz milk
- ½ tsp caster sugar
- 125g/4oz plain flour
- ½ tsp butter
- 5 tbsp chocolate sauce
- 250g/9oz chocolate chips
- 250g /9oz mini marshmallows
- 5 digestive biscuits

METHOD

1 Preheat the crepe maker whilst you crack the eggs into a bowl and beat with a fork. Stir in the milk and sugar. Sieve the flour into the mixture and whisk well or blend until a smooth lump-free batter is created.

2 Brush the heated crepe plate with butter before pouring on a thin layer of the mixture. Use a T-Stick or spreader to smooth the mixture evenly over the plate. Allow to cook for 60 seconds before gently flipping the crepe to cook the other side. Cook the other side for 60 seconds or until golden.

3 Repeat this cooking method for each crepe. Fold the crepes into quarters to serve. Drizzling across the crepes the chocolate sauce. Sprinkle the chocolate chips and mini marshmallows over the crepes and crumble the digestive biscuits on top to finish.

CHEFS NOTE

For a messy but melt in the mouth twist, pre-heat the chocolate chips & marshmallows in a pan or microwave before topping.

APPLE AND MAPLE SYRUP CREPE

Makes 5 crepes

INGREDIENTS

- 6 cooking apples
- 2 tbsp caster sugar
- 2 tsp cinnamon
- 2 free-range eggs
- 125g/4oz plain flour
- 200ml/7floz milk
- ½ tsp butter
- 5 tbsp maple syrup

CHEFS NOTE

Use as little or as much maple syrup as you please to satisfy your sweet tooth.

METHOD

1 Preheat the crepe maker and bring a small pan of water to boil, whilst you peel the cooking apples. Cut the apples into small cubes, disposing of the core and pips. Stew the apple for 10 minutes or until the apple is soft. Drain and place into a small bowl. Add the sugar and the cinnamon, gently mashing the mixture and place to one side ready to serve.

2 Crack the eggs into a bowl and beat with a fork. Stir in the milk and sieve the flour into the mixture, whisking well or blending until a smooth lump-free batter is created.

3 Brush the heated crepe plate with butter before pouring on a thin layer of the mixture. Use a T-Stick or spreader to smooth the mixture evenly over the plate. Allow to cook for 60 seconds before gently flipping the crepe to cook the other side. Cook the other side for 60 seconds or until golden.

4 Repeat this cooking method for each crepe. Fold the crepes into quarters to serve. Spoon the caramelised apple mixture on top of the pancakes and drizzle the maple syrup over to serve.

MANGO AND RASPBERRY CREPE

Makes 5 crepes

INGREDIENTS

- 250g/5oz raspberries
- 2 tbsp caster sugar
- 2 free-range eggs
- 175ml/6floz milk
- 25ml/1floz water
- 125g/4oz plain flour
- ½ tsp butter
- 250g/9oz mango, peeled and sliced

CHEFS NOTE

If you don't have much time, simply serve with whole raspberries and mango, crushing them with a fork will create a fresh, juicy topping without needing to caramelise.

METHOD

1 Preheat the crepe maker and bring a pan to heat. Add half of the raspberries into the pan and crush them up with a spoon or spatula. Mix in 1 tbsp sugar and stir well until a caramelised mixture is created. Place to one side and leave to cool.

2 Crack the eggs into a bowl and beat with a fork. Stir in the milk, water and the rest of the sugar. Sieve the flour into the mixture and whisk well or blend until a smooth lump-free batter is created.

3 Brush the heated crepe plate with butter before pouring on a thin layer of the mixture. Use a T-Stick or spreader to smooth the mixture evenly over the plate. Allow to cook for 60 seconds before gently flipping the crepe to cook the other side. Cook the other side for 60 seconds or until golden.

4 Repeat this cooking method for each crepe. Fold the crepes into quarters to serve. Peel and cut the mango into small cubes and serve on top of the crepes with the remaining raspberries. Drizzle over the raspberry mixture from the pan and serve.

BANANA SPLIT CREPE

Makes 5 crepes

INGREDIENTS

- 2 free-range eggs
- 200ml/7floz milk
- 1 tsp caster sugar
- 125g/4oz plain flour
- ½ tsp butter
- 5 bananas
- 2 tbsp whipped cream
- 150g/5oz raspberries
- Chocolate sauce to serve

METHOD

1 Preheat the crepe maker whilst you crack the eggs into a bowl and beat with a fork. Stir in the milk and sugar. Sieve the flour into the mixture and whisk well or blend until a smooth lump-free batter is created.

2 Brush the heated crepe plate with butter before pouring on a thin layer of the mixture. Use a T-Stick or spreader to smooth the mixture evenly over the plate. Allow to cook for 60 seconds before gently flipping the crepe to cook the other side. Cook the other side for 60 seconds or until golden.

3 Repeat this cooking method for each crepe. Peel the banana and place on top of the crepes to serve, slicing it length ways down the middle. Cover the banana in as much or as little whipped cream as you wish and drizzle across the chocolate sauce. Place the 5 raspberries on top ready to serve.

CHEFS NOTE

Mix this up as a winter warmer with hot sticky toffee sauce rather than chocolate.

TRADITIONAL SAVOURY CREPE

Makes 5 crepes

INGREDIENTS

- 2 free-range eggs
- 175ml/6floz milk
- 25ml/1floz water
- Pinch of Salt
- Pinch of Pepper
- 125g/4oz plain flour
- ½ tsp butter
- 3 large handfuls of rocket
- 5 tsp olive oil

METHOD

1 Preheat the crepe maker whilst you crack the eggs into a bowl and beat with a fork. Stir in the milk and water, along with the salt and pepper. Sieve the flour into the mixture and whisk well or blend until a smooth lump-free batter is created.

2 Brush the heated crepe plate with butter before pouring on a thin layer of the mixture. Use a T-Stick or spreader to smooth the mixture evenly over the plate. Allow to cook for 60 seconds before gently flipping the crepe to cook the other side. Cook the other side for 60 seconds or until golden.

3 Repeat this cooking method for each crepe. Serve with a side of fresh rocket leaves drizzled in olive oil or your choice of topping.

CHEFS NOTE

Drizzle the olive oil over the rocket leaves earlier in the day and leave to chill in the fridge - the nice, cold salad will provide a delicious contrast to the warmly served crepes.

TOMATO AND PESTO CREPE

Makes 5 crepes

INGREDIENTS

- 2 free-range eggs
- 175ml/6floz milk
- 25ml/1floz water
- Pinch of salt
- Pinch of pepper
- 125g/4oz plain flour
- ½ tsp butter
- 250g/9oz cherry tomatoes
- 5 tbsp green pesto

METHOD

1 Preheat the crepe maker whilst you crack the eggs into a bowl and beat with a fork. Stir in the milk and water, along with the salt and pepper. Sieve the flour into the mixture and whisk well or blend until a smooth lump-free batter is created.

2 Brush the heated crepe plate with butter before pouring on a thin layer of the mixture. Use a T-Stick or spreader to smooth the mixture evenly over the plate. Allow to cook for 60 seconds before gently flipping the crepe to cook the other side. Cook the other side for 60 seconds or until golden.

3 Repeat this cooking method for each crepe. Fold the crepes ready to serve. Slice the cherry tomatoes in half and scatter over the crepes. Spoon over the green pesto and enjoy.

CHEFS NOTE

Serve with fresh salad leaves for extra flavour and texture.

SMOKED SALMON CREPE

Makes 5 crepes

INGREDIENTS

- 2 free-range eggs
- 200ml/7floz milk
- Pinch of salt
- Pinch of pepper
- 125g/4oz plain flour
- ½ tsp butter
- 250g/9oz smoked salmon
- 5 tbsp cream cheese
- Large bunch freshly chopped dill
- Freshly ground black pepper

METHOD

1 Preheat the crepe maker whilst you crack the eggs into a bowl and beat with a fork. Stir in the milk and the salt and pepper. Sieve the flour into the mixture and whisk well or blend until a smooth lump-free batter is created.

2 Brush the heated crepe plate with butter before pouring on a thin layer of the mixture. Use a T-Stick or spreader to smooth the mixture evenly over the plate. Allow to cook for 60 seconds before gently flipping the crepe to cook the other side. Cook the other side for 60 seconds or until golden.

3 Repeat this cooking method for each crepe. Fold the crepes into quarters ready to serve. Finely cut the smoked salmon and serve on top of the crepes along with the cream cheese. Finely chop the Dill and sprinkle over the salmon & cream cheese along with a little black pepper.

CHEFS NOTE

Freshly cut dill provides a light, fresh flavour.

BACON AND AVOCADO CREPE

Makes 5 crepes

INGREDIENTS

- 5 slices back bacon
- 2 free-range eggs
- 200ml/7floz milk
- Pinch of salt
- Pinch of pepper
- 125g/4oz plain flour
- ½ tsp butter
- 2 large ripe avocados
- Freshly ground black pepper

CHEFS NOTE

Use more bacon and/ or avocado as you please; pancetta can work equally well instead of bacon

METHOD

1 Preheat the crepe maker whilst you either fry or grill the bacon. Crack the eggs into a bowl and beat with a fork. Stir in the milk and the salt and pepper. Sieve the flour into the mixture and whisk well or blend until a smooth lump-free batter is created.

2 Once the bacon is cooked, cut it into small pieces to achieve a 'shredded' effect and place to one side ready to shortly serve.

3 Brush the heated crepe plate with butter before pouring on a thin layer of the mixture. Use a T-Stick or spreader to smooth the mixture evenly over the plate. Allow to cook for 60 seconds before gently flipping the crepe to cook the other side. Cook the other side for 60 seconds or until golden.

4 Repeat this cooking method for each crepe. Fold the crepes into quarters and add the finely cut bacon on top. Chop the avocado into small cubes and add to the bacon along with some ground black pepper.

VERY BRITISH CHEESE & CUCUMBER CREPE

Makes 5 crepes

INGREDIENTS

- 1 whole cucumber
- 2 free-range eggs
- 200ml/7floz milk
- Pinch of salt
- Pinch of pepper
- 125g/4oz plain flour
- ½ tsp butter
- 5 tbsp cream cheese
- Freshly ground black pepper

CHEFS NOTE

A quick squeeze of fresh lime juice can add a delicious, zesty finish to this recipe.

METHOD

1 Preheat the crepe maker whilst you prepare the cucumber for topping: cut a few slices of the cucumber and place to one side to serve alongside the crepe as garnish; cut the remainder of the cucumber into long strips and finely slice the cucumber into thin pieces, creating a 'shredded' effect. Move to the side to serve on top of the crepe.

2 Crack the eggs into a bowl and beat with a fork. Stir in the milk and the salt and pepper. Sieve the flour into the mixture and whisk well or blend until a smooth lump-free batter is created.

3 Brush the heated crepe plate with butter before pouring on a thin layer of the mixture. Use a T-Stick or spreader to smooth the mixture evenly over the plate. Allow to cook for 60 seconds before gently flipping the crepe to cook the other side. Cook the other side for 60 seconds or until golden.

4 Repeat this cooking method for each crepe. Fold the crepes into quarters and sprinkle on top the shredded cucumber and ground black pepper. Spoon the cream cheese on top, or on the side if you prefer, and serve.

GARLIC MUSHROOM CREPE

Makes 5 crepes

INGREDIENTS

- 1 tsp olive oil
- 250g/9oz button mushrooms, chopped
- 2 cloves of garlic, crushed
- 2 free-range eggs
- 175ml/6floz milk
- 25ml/1floz water
- Pinch of salt
- Pinch of pepper
- 125g/4oz plain flour
- ½ tsp butter

CHEFS NOTE

Add a pinch of fresh mixed herbs to serve.

METHOD

1 Preheat the crepe maker whilst you bring a pan to heat. Drizzle the olive oil into the pan. Finely cut the mushrooms and crush the garlic, adding both into the pan and cook for 5 minutes or until golden brown. Once cooked, bring off the heat and place to one side to shortly serve.

2 Crack the eggs into a bowl and beat with a fork. Stir in the milk and water, along with the salt and pepper. Sieve the flour into the mixture and whisk well or blend until a smooth lump-free batter is created.

3 Brush the heated crepe plate with butter before pouring on a thin layer of the mixture. Use a T-Stick or spreader to smooth the mixture evenly over the plate. Allow to cook for 60 seconds before gently flipping the crepe to cook the other side. Cook the other side for 60 seconds or until golden.

4 Repeat this cooking method for each crepe. Fold the crepes into quarters and spoon on top the garlic mushroom mixture ready to serve.

SIMPLE CHEESY CREPE

Makes 5 crepes

INGREDIENTS

- 2 free-range eggs
- 200ml/7floz milk
- Pinch of salt
- Pinch of pepper
- 125g/4oz plain flour
- ½ tsp butter
- 250g/5oz cheddar cheese, finely grated

METHOD

1 Preheat the crepe maker whilst you crack the eggs into a bowl and beat with a fork. Stir in the milk and the salt and pepper. Sieve the flour into the mixture and whisk well or blend until a smooth lump-free batter is created.

2 Brush the heated crepe plate with butter before pouring on a thin layer of the mixture. Use a T-Stick or spreader to smooth the mixture evenly over the plate. Allow to cook for 60 seconds before gently flipping the crepe to cook the other side. Cook the other side for 60 seconds or until golden.

3 Repeat this cooking method for each crepe. Fold the crepes ready to serve and sprinkle on top the grated cheese, allowing the cheese to melt slightly before enjoying.

CHEFS NOTE

Serve with mixed salad leaves and fresh tomatoes or try with a spoonful of green pesto or sundried tomato pesto.

CHOCOLATE COFFEE CREPE

Makes 5 crepes

INGREDIENTS

- 2 free-range eggs
- 175ml/6floz milk
- 25ml/1floz water
- Pinch of salt
- Pinch of pepper
- 125g/4oz plain flour
- ½ tsp butter
- 5 tbsp cocoa powder
- 2 tsp ground Coffee
- 5 tbsp chocolate sauce
- Whole coffee beans to serve

CHEFS NOTE

Experiment with dark chocolate for a richer taste.

METHOD

1 Preheat the crepe maker whilst you crack the eggs into a bowl and beat with a fork. Stir in the milk and water along with the salt and pepper. Sieve the flour into the mixture and whisk well or blend until a smooth lump-free batter is created.

2 Brush the heated crepe plate with butter before pouring on a thin layer of the mixture. Use a T-Stick or spreader to smooth the mixture evenly over the plate. Allow to cook for 60 seconds before gently flipping the crepe to cook the other side. Cook the other side for 60 seconds or until golden.

3 Repeat this cooking method for each crepe. Fold the crepes into quarters ready to serve. Mix the cocoa powder and powdered coffee together and dust over the crepes.

4 Squeeze as much or as little chocolate sauce on top as well, and add the coffee beans on top for decoration.

PINE NUT AND MANGO CREPE

Makes 5 crepes

INGREDIENTS

- 250g/9oz mango, peeled & cubed
- 2 free-range eggs
- 175ml/6floz milk
- 25ml/1floz water
- Pinch of salt
- Pinch of pepper
- 125g/4oz plain flour
- ½ tsp butter
- 5 tbsp pine nuts

CHEFS NOTE

Mix 1 tsp of freshly squeezed lime juice with 2 tsp of olive oil for a delicious dressing to accompany.

METHOD

1 Preheat the crepe maker whilst you prepare the mango ready for later: peel and cut the mango into small cubes removing any core and place to one side ready to shortly serve.

2 Crack the eggs into a bowl and beat with a fork. Stir in the milk and water along with the salt and pepper. Sieve the flour into the mixture and whisk well or blend until a smooth lump-free batter is created.

3 Brush the heated crepe plate with butter before pouring on a thin layer of the mixture. Use a T-Stick or spreader to smooth the mixture evenly over the plate. Allow to cook for 60 seconds before gently flipping the crepe to cook the other side. Cook the other side for 60 seconds or until golden.

4 Repeat this cooking method for each crepe. Fold the crepes into quarters and add the mango on top. Sprinkle over the pine nuts and serve.

SPINACH AND RICOTTA CREPE

Makes 5 crepes

INGREDIENTS

- 3 large handfuls of fresh spinach
- 2 free-range eggs
- 175ml/6floz milk
- 25ml/1fl oz water
- Pinch of salt
- Pinch of pepper
- 125g/4oz plain flour
- ½ tsp butter
- 5 tbsp ricotta cheese
- Freshly ground black pepper

METHOD

1 Preheat the crepe maker whilst you bring a pan of water to boil. Add the spinach leaves into the pan and cook for a few minutes until the leaves begin to soft and wilt. Drain the spinach and place to one side to shortly serve.

2 Crack the eggs into a bowl and beat with a fork. Stir in the milk and water along with the salt and pepper. Sieve the flour into the mixture and whisk well or blend until a smooth lump-free batter is created.

3 Brush the heated crepe plate with butter before pouring on a thin layer of the mixture. Use a T-Stick or spreader to smooth the mixture evenly over the plate. Allow to cook for 60 seconds before gently flipping the crepe to cook the other side. Cook the other side for 60 seconds or until golden.

4 Repeat this cooking method for each crepe. Fold the crepes into quarters and top with the cooked spinach. Serve with a spoonful of ricotta cheese and enjoy with some freshly ground black pepper.

CHEFS NOTE

Add a drizzle of garlic olive oil or a little pinch of freshly crushed garlic for a twist on this recipe.

CHEESY LEEK CREPE

Makes 5 crepes

INGREDIENTS

- 1 tsp olive oil
- 3 leeks, sliced
- 3 tbsp double cream
- 20g/7oz cheddar cheese, grated
- 2 free-range eggs
- 175ml/6floz milk
- 25ml/1floz water
- Pinch of salt
- Pinch of pepper
- 125g/4oz plain flour
- ½ tsp butter
- 3 tbsp pine nuts

CHEFS NOTE

For a lighter version, try using a low-fat Crème Fraiche instead of Double Cream.

METHOD

1 Preheat the crepe maker and bring a pan to heat. Drizzle in the olive oil and finely cut the leeks. Add the leeks into the pan and cook for 2-3 minutes or until it begins to soften and turn golden brown, stirring throughout. Add the cream and cheese to the leeks and reduce to a low heat. Stir until a nice mixture is created and the cheese is melted. Keep on a low heat, stirring occasionally while you prepare the crepe mixture.

2 Crack the eggs into a bowl and beat with a fork. Stir in the milk and water along with the salt and pepper. Sieve the flour into the mixture and whisk well or blend until a smooth lump-free batter is created.

3 Brush the heated crepe plate with butter before pouring on a thin layer of the mixture. Use a T-Stick or spreader to smooth the mixture evenly over the plate. Allow to cook for 60 seconds before gently flipping the crepe to cook the other side. Cook the other side for 60 seconds or until golden.

4 Repeat this cooking method for each crepe. Fold the crepes into quarters and pour on top the creamy leek mixture ready to serve.

SUPER EASY PEANUT BUTTER CREPE

Makes 5 crepes

INGREDIENTS

- 2 eggs
- 200ml/7fl oz milk
- Pinch of salt
- Pinch of pepper
- 125g/4oz plain flour
- ½ tsp butter
- 5 tbsp smooth peanut butter
- 5 tsp peanuts, crushed

METHOD

1 Preheat the crepe maker whilst you crack the eggs into a bowl and beat with a fork. Stir in the milk and salt and pepper. Sieve the flour into the mixture and whisk well or blend until a smooth lump-free batter is created.

2 Brush the heated crepe plate with butter before pouring on a thin layer of the mixture. Use a T-Stick or spreader to smooth the mixture evenly over the plate. Allow to cook for 60 seconds before gently flipping the crepe to cook the other side. Cook the other side for 60 seconds or until golden.

3 Repeat this cooking method for each crepe. Fold the crepes into quarters and serve with a spoonful of peanut butter. Sprinkle on top the crushed peanuts ready to serve.

CHEFS NOTE

Serve with as little or as much peanut butter as you prefer; try spreading the peanut butter across the crepes for balanced flavour.

TRADITIONAL CREPE COMPOTES & SAUCES

SWEET CREPES WITH RASPBERRY COULIS

Makes 5 crepes

INGREDIENTS

- 200g/7oz raspberries
- 1 tbsp water
- 1 tbsp caster sugar
- 1 tsp vanilla extract
- 2 free-range eggs
- 175ml/6floz milk
- 25ml/1floz water
- 125g/4oz plain flour
- ½ tsp butter

CHEFS NOTE

Serve with a wedge of lemon to add a zesty burst of flavour to your crepe.

METHOD

1 Preheat the crepe maker whilst you bring a pan to heat. Cut the raspberries into halves or quarters and add to the pan along with the water, 2 tsp caster sugar and vanilla extract. Sauté until the raspberries begin to soften and break down into a lumpy coulis mixture. Once cooked, sieve the mixture to remove seeds or if you prefer just leave to one side to use as it is.

2 Crack the eggs into a bowl and beat with a fork. Stir in the milk, water and remaining sugar. Sieve the flour into the mixture and whisk well or blend until a smooth lump-free batter is created.

3 Brush the heated crepe plate with butter before pouring on a thin layer of the mixture. Use a T-Stick or spreader to smooth the mixture evenly over the plate. Allow to cook for 60 seconds before gently flipping the crepe to cook the other side. Cook the other side for 60 seconds or until golden.

4 Repeat this cooking method for each crepe. Fold or roll the crepes to serve and drizzle with the raspberry coulis.

SWEET CREPES WITH PEACH COMPOTE

Makes 5 crepes

INGREDIENTS

- 4 peaches
- 1 tsp water
- 1 tbsp caster sugar
- Squeeze of lemon juice
- 2 free-range eggs
- 175ml/6floz milk
- 25ml/1floz water
- 125g/4oz plain flour
- ½ tsp butter

CHEFS NOTE

Serve with a spoonful of fresh cream or drizzle in honey too.

METHOD

1 Preheat the crepe maker whilst you bring a pan to heat. Peel and de-stone the peaches before cutting into small cubes. Add the peach cubes, water, 2 tsp sugar and a squeeze of lemon juice into the pan and gently cook for 4-5 minutes. Sauté until the peaches begin to soften and dissolve into a compote mixture. Remove from the heat and place to one side.

2 Crack the eggs into a bowl and beat with a fork. Stir in the milk, water and remaining sugar. Sieve the flour into the mixture and whisk well or blend until a smooth lump-free batter is created.

3 Brush the heated crepe plate with butter before pouring on a thin layer of the mixture. Use a T-Stick or spreader to smooth the mixture evenly over the plate. Allow to cook for 60 seconds before gently flipping the crepe to cook the other side. Cook the other side for 60 seconds or until golden.

4 Repeat this cooking method for each crepe. Fold or roll the crepes to serve and drizzle with the peach compote.

SWEET CREPES WITH CHOCOLATE SYRUP

Makes 5 crepes

INGREDIENTS

- 50g/2oz cocoa powder
- 225ml/8floz water
- 50ml/2floz milk
- 50g/2oz caster sugar
- 2 free-range eggs
- 125g/4oz plain flour
- ½ tsp butter

METHOD

1 Preheat the crepe maker whilst you bring a pan to heat. Add into the pan the cocoa powder, 50ml of the water and 25ml of the milk and sugar. Stir on a medium heat until the ingredients have dissolved into each other. Continue to stir for 3-4 minutes or until the liquid begins to thicken into a syrup-like consistency. Remove from the heat and place to one side.

2 Crack the eggs into a bowl and beat with a fork. Stir in the remaining milk and water as well as a pinch of sugar. Sieve the flour into the mixture and whisk well or blend until a smooth lump-free batter is created.

3 Brush the heated crepe plate with butter before pouring on a thin layer of the mixture. Use a T-Stick or spreader to smooth the mixture evenly over the plate. Allow to cook for 60 seconds before gently flipping the crepe to cook the other side. Cook the other side for 60 seconds or until golden.

4 Repeat this cooking method for each crepe. Fold or roll the crepes to serve and drizzle the chocolate syrup over the top.

CHEFS NOTE

For those chocoholics try serving with milk chocolate chunks for an even sweeter crepe.

SWEET CREPES WITH MINTED STRAWBERRY

Makes 5 crepes

INGREDIENTS

- 250g/9oz strawberries
- Small bunch fresh mint leaves, finely chopped
- 2 tbsp icing sugar
- 1 tsp vanilla extract
- 2 free-range eggs
- 175ml/6floz milk
- 25ml/1floz water
- 1 tsp caster sugar
- 125g/4oz plain flour
- ½ tsp butter

CHEFS NOTE

For a warm compote, warm the minted strawberry mixture thoroughly in a pan, before serving.

METHOD

1 Preheat the crepe maker whilst you prepare the strawberry compote. Remove the stalks and leaves from the strawberries and cut quarters. Along with the finely chopped mint leaves, icing sugar and vanilla essence, lightly blend the strawberries until a lumpy mixture is created. Place to one side.

2 Crack the eggs into a bowl and beat with a fork. Stir in the milk, water and sugar. Sieve the flour into the mixture and whisk well or blend until a smooth lump-free batter is created.

3 Brush the heated crepe plate with butter before pouring on a thin layer of the mixture. Use a T-Stick or spreader to smooth the mixture evenly over the plate. Allow to cook for 60 seconds before gently flipping the crepe to cook the other side. Cook the other side for 60 seconds or until golden.

4 Repeat this cooking method for each crepe. Fold or roll the crepes to serve and spoon on the minted strawberry compote. Add a mint leaf or two for decoration to serve if desired.

SWEET CREPES WITH SPICED PEAR COMPOTE

Makes 5 crepes

INGREDIENTS

- 4 pears
- 2 tbsp icing sugar
- 1 tsp brown sugar
- ½ tsp cinnamon, ground
- 1 tsp vanilla extract
- Squeeze of orange juice
- 2 free-range eggs
- 175ml/6floz milk
- 25ml/1floz water
- 1 tsp caster sugar
- 125g/4oz plain flour
- ½ tsp butter

CHEFS NOTE

Adding a dash of brandy to this compote can make a real winter warmer.

METHOD

1 Preheat the crepe maker whilst you heat a pan. Peel the pears, removing the core and cut into cubes. Add the pear cubes along with the icing sugar, brown sugar, cinnamon and vanilla extract into the pan. Add a quick squeeze of orange juice and stir well. Keep on a medium heat for 4-5 minutes or until the pears begin to break down and the sugars dissolve. Remove from the heat and place to one side.

2 Crack the eggs into a bowl and beat with a fork. Stir in the milk, water and caster sugar. Sieve the flour into the mixture and whisk well or blend until a smooth lump-free batter is created.

3 Brush the heated crepe plate with butter before pouring on a thin layer of the mixture. Use a T-Stick or spreader to smooth the mixture evenly over the plate. Allow to cook for 60 seconds before gently flipping the crepe to cook the other side. Cook the other side for 60 seconds or until golden.

4 Repeat this cooking method for each crepe. Fold or roll the crepes to serve and spoon on top the spiced pear compote.

SWEET CREPES WITH SALTED CARAMEL SYRUP

Makes 5 crepes

INGREDIENTS

- 125g/4oz butter
- 375g/13oz brown sugar
- 450ml/15½ floz double cream
- 1 tsp vanilla extract
- 1 large pinch of salt
- 2 free-range eggs
- 175ml/6floz milk
- 25ml/1floz water
- 1 tsp caster sugar
- 125g/4oz plain flour
- ½ tsp butter

CHEFS NOTE

Top with some caramel chunks or chocolate chips or simply enjoy it as it is.

METHOD

1 Preheat the crepe maker whilst you bring a pan to heat. Melt the butter in the pan and gradually pour in the brown sugar and cream. Stir well and add in the vanilla extract and salt. Allow the mixture to come to boil, stirring or swirling occasionally. Once the sugar has all dissolved, remove from the heat and place the syrup to one side.

2 Crack the eggs into a bowl and beat with a fork. Stir in the milk, water and caster sugar. Sieve the flour into the mixture and whisk well or blend until a smooth lump-free batter is created.

3 Brush the heated crepe plate with butter before pouring on a thin layer of the mixture. Use a T-Stick or spreader to smooth the mixture evenly over the plate. Allow to cook for 60 seconds before gently flipping the crepe to cook the other side. Cook the other side for 60 seconds or until golden.

4 Repeat this cooking method for each crepe. Fold or roll the crepes to serve and drizzle over the salted caramel syrup and enjoy.

SWEET CREPES WITH STICKY TOFFEE SAUCE

Makes 5 crepes

INGREDIENTS

- 125g/4oz butter
- 375g/13oz brown sugar
- 400ml/14floz double cream
- 150g/5oz golden syrup
- 1 tsp vanilla extract
- 2 free-range eggs
- 175ml/6floz milk
- 25ml/1floz water
- 1 tsp caster sugar
- 125g/4oz plain flour
- ½ tsp butter

CHEFS NOTE

Use soft brown sugar if you can as it dissolved a lot quicker than normal brown sugar.

METHOD

1 Preheat the crepe maker whilst you bring a pan to heat. Melt the butter in the pan and gradually pour in the brown sugar, cream, golden syrup and vanilla extract. Stir the mixture on a medium heat until it blends well, allowing the sugar and syrup to dissolve into a thick sauce. Allow the mixture to come to boil, stirring or swirling occasionally and then remove from the heat and place to one side.

2 Crack the eggs into a bowl and beat with a fork. Stir in the milk, water and caster sugar. Sieve the flour into the mixture and whisk well or blend until a smooth lump-free batter is created.

3 Brush the heated crepe plate with butter before pouring on a thin layer of the mixture. Use a T-Stick or spreader to smooth the mixture evenly over the plate. Allow to cook for 60 seconds before gently flipping the crepe to cook the other side. Cook the other side for 60 seconds or until golden.

4 Repeat this cooking method for each crepe. Fold or roll the crepes and pour over the hot sticky toffee sauce to serve.

SWEET CREPES WITH BLACKBERRY COULIS

Makes 5 crepes

INGREDIENTS

- 200g/7oz blackberries
- 2 tbsp water
- 1 tbsp caster sugar
- 2 tsp icing sugar
- 1 tsp vanilla extract
- 2 free-range eggs
- 175ml/6floz milk
- 25ml/1floz water
- 125g/4oz plain flour
- ½ tsp butter

CHEFS NOTE

Serve with a generous spoonful of ice cream.

METHOD

1 Preheat the crepe maker whilst you bring a pan to heat. Cut the blackberries into halves or quarters and add to the pan along with the water, 2 tsp of caster sugar, icing sugar and vanilla extract.

2 Sauté until the blackberries begin to soften and break down into a lumpy coulis mixture. Once cooked, sieve the mixture to remove seeds or if you prefer, just leave to one side to serve as it is.

3 Crack the eggs into a bowl and beat with a fork. Stir in the milk, water and remaining sugar. Sieve the flour into the mixture and whisk well or blend until a smooth lump-free batter is created.

4 Brush the heated crepe plate with butter before pouring on a thin layer of the mixture. Use a T-Stick or spreader to smooth the mixture evenly over the plate. Allow to cook for 60 seconds before gently flipping the crepe to cook the other side. Cook the other side for 60 seconds or until golden.

5 Repeat this cooking method for each crepe. Fold or roll the crepes to serve and spoon on the blackberry coulis.

SAVOURY CREPES WITH HOLLANDAISE SAUCE

Makes 5 crepes

INGREDIENTS

- 200g/7oz butter
- 4 free-range egg yolks
- 2 tsp white wine vinegar
- 1 tsp peppercorns, ground
- A squeeze of fresh lemon juice
- 2 free-range eggs
- 175ml/6floz milk
- 25ml/1floz water
- Pinch of salt
- Pinch of pepper
- 125g/4oz plain flour
- ½ tsp butter

METHOD

1 Preheat the crepe maker whilst you begin to simmer small pan of water. In a glass bowl, add the egg yolks, white wine vinegar, pepper and a pinch of salt and mix well.

2 Place the bowl over the pan of simmering water and whisk well and continuously to blend the ingredients and thicken the sauce. Bring another pan to heat and begin melting the butter. Once the sauce is thickened, add in with the butter and combine the butter with the sauce. Add a squeeze of lemon juice, stir, and keep on a low heat until serving. Be careful not to burn the sauce and continue to stir whilst preparing the crepes.

3 Crack the 2 eggs into a bowl and beat with a fork. Stir in the milk and water, along with the salt and pepper. Sieve the flour into the mixture and whisk well or blend until a smooth lump-free batter is created.

4 Brush the heated crepe plate with butter before pouring on a thin layer of the mixture. Use a T-Stick or spreader to smooth the mixture evenly over the plate. Allow to cook for 60 seconds before gently flipping the crepe to cook the other side. Cook the other side for 60 seconds or until golden.

5 Repeat this cooking method for each crepe. Fold or roll the crepes and pour on the Hollandaise sauce to serve.

CHEFS NOTE

Serve with freshly chopped parsley. If the sauce thickens too much, add a small amount of water and mix. Repeat until you reach the right consistency.

SAVOURY CREPES WITH BÉCHAMEL SAUCE

Makes 5 crepes

INGREDIENTS

- 50g/2oz butter
- 175g/6oz plain flour
- 600ml /1 pint full fat milk
- ½ tsp nutmeg, grated
- 1 tsp salt
- 2 free-range eggs
- 175ml/6floz milk
- 25ml/1floz water
- Pinch of salt
- Pinch of pepper
- ½ tsp butter

CHEFS NOTE

Feel free to add more pepper or nutmeg to suit your taste buds. If serving for guests, sprinkle some whole peppercorns on top for decoration to serve.

METHOD

1 Preheat the crepe maker whilst you begin to melt the butter in a pan. Once the butter has melted, add in 50g of the flour and whisk until a lump-free mixture is achieved. Continue to stir over a medium heat for 4-5 minutes, or until the mixture turns golden in colour.

2 In a second pan, bring the milk to boil. Once it reaches boiliong point, gradually add the milk into the butter and flour mixture, whisking continuously. When the two have combined, add in the finely grated nutmeg and salt and whisk well again. Keep on a low heat until serving. Be careful not to burn the sauce and continue to stir whilst preparing the crepes.

3 Crack the 2 eggs into a bowl and beat with a fork. Stir in the milk and water, along with the salt and pepper. Sieve the flour into the mixture and whisk well or blend until a smooth lump-free batter is created.

4 Brush the heated crepe plate with butter before pouring on a thin layer of the mixture. Use a T-Stick or spreader to smooth the mixture evenly over the plate. Allow to cook for 60 secs before gently flipping the crepe to cook the other side. Cook the other side for 60 secs or until golden.

5 Repeat this cooking method for each crepe. Fold or roll the crepes and pour on t Béchamel sauce to serve.

CREPE VARIETIES

SIMPLE VEGAN SWEET CREPES

Makes 5 crepes

INGREDIENTS

- 175ml /6floz soy milk
- 25ml /1floz water
- 1 tsp vanilla extract
- 125g /4oz plain flour
- ½ tsp soy butter
- Lemon wedge and sugar for serving

METHOD

1 Preheat the crepe maker whilst you mix the soy milk, water and vanilla extract together in a bowl. Sieve the flour into the mixture and whisk well or blend until a smooth lump-free batter is created.

2 Brush the heated crepe plate with the soy butter before pouring on a thin layer of the mixture. Use a T-Stick or spreader to smooth the mixture evenly over the plate. Allow to cook for 60 seconds before gently flipping the crepe to cook the other side. Cook the other side for 60 seconds or until golden.

3 Repeat this cooking method for each crepe. Drizzle with freshly squeezed lemon juice and sugar and/or the topping of your choice.

CHEFS NOTE

You can also make these without the vanilla extract if you wish to keep things even simpler.

SIMPLE VEGAN SAVOURY CREPES

Makes 5 crepes

INGREDIENTS

- 175ml/6floz soy milk
- 25ml /1floz water
- Pinch of salt
- Pinch of pepper
- 125g/4oz plain flour
- ½ tsp soy butter

METHOD

1 Preheat the crepe maker whilst you mix the soy milk, water, salt and pepper together in a bowl. Sieve the flour into the mixture and whisk well or blend until a smooth lump-free batter is created.

2 Brush the heated crepe plate with the soy butter before pouring on a thin layer of the mixture. Use a T-Stick or spreader to smooth the mixture evenly over the plate. Allow to cook for 60 seconds before gently flipping the crepe to cook the other side. Cook the other side for 60 seconds or until golden.

3 Repeat this cooking method for each crepe. Serve with a side of fresh dressed salad leaves or your choice of savoury topping.

CHEFS NOTE

You could also try using almond or coconut butter instead of soy butter.

GOOD FOR YOU DAIRY-FREE CREPES

Makes 5 crepes

INGREDIENTS

- 2 free-range eggs
- 175ml/6floz almond milk
- 25ml /1floz water
- 125g/4oz wholegrain flour
- 1 tsp of Sugar
- ½ tsp almond Butter

METHOD

1 Preheat the crepe maker whilst you crack the eggs into a bowl. Whisk the eggs and gradually add in the almond milk and water. Stir well.

2 Sieve the flour into the mixture, add the sugar then whisk well or blend until a smooth lump-free batter is created.

3 Brush the heated crepe plate with the almond butter before pouring on a thin layer of the mixture. Use a T-Stick or spreader to smooth the mixture evenly over the plate. Allow to cook for 60 seconds before gently flipping the crepe to cook the other side. Cook the other side for 60 seconds or until golden.

4 Repeat this cooking method for each crepe. Roll or fold and serve with your topping or side of choice.

CHEFS NOTE

Swap the almond milk and almond butter for soy to keep flavours simple for adding in your filling or topping of choice.

SUPER SIMPLE VEGAN CREPES

Makes 5 crepes

INGREDIENTS

- 125g/4oz plain flour
- 330ml/12floz sparkling water
- ½ tsp soy butter

METHOD

1 Preheat the crepe maker whilst you sieve the flour into the sparkling water and either whisk well or blend until a smooth lump-free batter is created.

2 Brush the heated crepe plate with soy butter before pouring on a thin layer of the mixture. Use a T-Stick or spreader to smooth the mixture evenly over the plate. Allow to cook for 40 seconds before gently flipping the crepe to cook the other side. Cook the other side for 40 seconds or until golden.

3 Repeat this cooking method for each crepe. Fold or roll the crepes to serve.

CHEFS NOTE

Try using a flavoured sparkling water to experiment with different tastes.

ELDERFLOWER CREPE

Makes 5 crepes

INGREDIENTS

- 2 free-range eggs
- 150ml/5floz milk
- 25ml/1floz sparkling water
- 25ml/1floz elderflower cordial
- 125g/4oz plain flour
- ½ tsp butter

METHOD

1 Preheat the crepe maker whilst you crack the eggs into a bowl and beat with a fork. Stir in the milk, sparkling water and elderflower cordial. Sieve the flour into the mixture and whisk well or blend until a smooth lump-free batter is created.

2 Brush the heated crepe plate with butter before pouring on a thin layer of the mixture. Use a T-Stick or spreader to smooth the mixture evenly over the plate. Allow to cook for 60 seconds before gently flipping the crepe to cook the other side. Cook the other side for 60 seconds or until golden.

3 Repeat this cooking method for each crepe. Fold or roll each crepe to serve.

CHEFS NOTE

Drizzle some freshly squeezed lime juice on top to compliment the Elderflower.

BRILLIANT BEER CREPES

Makes 5 crepes

INGREDIENTS

- 2 free-range eggs
- 150ml/5floz milk
- 50ml/2floz beer
- 125g/4oz plain flour
- A pinch of salt
- ½ tsp butter

METHOD

1 Preheat the crepe maker whilst you crack the eggs into a bowl and beat with a fork. Stir in the milk and beer or lager. Sieve the flour into the mixture and add the pinch of salt. Whisk well or blend until a smooth lump-free batter is created.

2 Brush the heated crepe plate with butter before pouring on a thin layer of the mixture. Use a T-Stick or spreader to smooth the mixture evenly over the plate. Allow to cook for 60 seconds before gently flipping the crepe to cook the other side. Cook the other side for 60 seconds or until golden.

3 Repeat this cooking method for each crepe. Fold or roll each crepe ready to serve.

CHEFS NOTE

These go surprisingly well with chocolate inspired toppings and fillings!

BOOZY BLACKCURRANT CREPES

Makes 5 crepes

INGREDIENTS

- 2 free-range eggs
- 175ml/6floz milk
- 25ml/1floz 1ater
- 1 tbsp crème de cassis
- 125g/4oz plain flour
- ½ tsp butter
- Fresh blackcurrants to serve
- Icing sugar for dusting

METHOD

1 Preheat the crepe maker whilst you crack the eggs into a bowl and beat with a fork. Stir in the milk, water and crème de cassis. Sieve the flour into the mixture and whisk well or blend until a smooth lump-free batter is created.

2 Brush the heated crepe plate with butter before pouring on a thin layer of the mixture. Use a T-Stick or spreader to smooth the mixture evenly over the plate. Allow to cook for 60 seconds before gently flipping the crepe to cook the other side. Cook the other side for 60 seconds or until golden.

3 Repeat this cooking method for each crepe. Fold or roll the crepes to serve and top with fresh blackcurrants & a dusting of icing sugar.

CHEFS NOTE

A large spoonful of freshly whipped cream sets this off a treat.

GLUTEN-FREE CREPES

Makes 5 crepes

INGREDIENTS

- 2 free-range eggs
- 175ml/6floz milk
- 25ml/1floz water
- ½ tsp vanilla extract
- 1 tsp Sugar
- 125g/4oz potato flour
- ½ tsp Butter
- Lemon wedges and sugar for serving

METHOD

1 Preheat the crepe maker whilst you crack the eggs in a bowl and whisk. Mix in the milk, water, vanilla extract and sugar. Sieve the potato flour into the mixture and whisk well or blend until a smooth lump-free batter is created.

2 Brush the heated crepe plate with the butter before pouring on a thin layer of the mixture. Use a T-Stick or spreader to smooth the mixture evenly over the plate. Allow to cook for 60 seconds before gently flipping the crepe to cook the other side. Cook the other side for 60 seconds or until golden.

3 Repeat this cooking method for each crepe. Drizzle with freshly squeezed lemon juice and sugar and/or the topping of your choice.

CHEFS NOTE

A pinch of salt and pepper rather than sugar and vanilla can make these savoury. Rice flour is also a great gluten free substitute in crepes.

QUINOA CREPES

Makes 5 crepes

INGREDIENTS

- 2 free-range eggs
- 175ml/6floz milk
- 25ml/1floz water
- A pinch of salt
- 125g/4oz quinoa flour
- ½ tsp butter
- Honey for serving

METHOD

1 Preheat the crepe maker whilst you crack the eggs in a bowl and whisk. Mix in the milk and water & add a pinch of salt. Sieve the quinoa flour into the mixture and whisk well or blend until a smooth lump-free batter is created.

2 Brush the heated crepe plate with the butter before pouring on a thin layer of the mixture. Use a T-Stick or spreader to smooth the mixture evenly over the plate. Allow to cook for 60 seconds before gently flipping the crepe to cook the other side. Cook the other side for 60 seconds or until golden.

3 Repeat this cooking method for each crepe. Fold or roll the crepes to serve and drizzle over honey or your choice of topping.

CHEFS NOTE

Quinoa crepes work fantastically with savoury fillings – they're gluten free too!

CHOCOLATE CREPES

Makes 5 crepes

INGREDIENTS

- 2 free-range eggs
- 200ml/7floz milk
- 1 tsp vanilla extract
- 1 tsp sugar
- 100g/3½oz flour
- 25g/1oz cocoa powder
- ½ tsp butter
- Icing sugar for serving

METHOD

1 Preheat the crepe maker whilst you crack the eggs in a bowl and whisk. Mix in the milk, vanilla extract and sugar. Sieve the flour and cocoa powder into the mixture, whisk well or blend until a smooth lump-free batter is created.

2 Brush the heated crepe plate with the butter before pouring on a thin layer of the mixture. Use a T-Stick or spreader to smooth the mixture evenly over the plate. Allow to cook for 60 seconds before gently flipping the crepe to cook the other side. Cook the other side for 60 seconds or until golden.

3 Repeat this cooking method for each crepe. Fold or roll each crepe and dust over the icing sugar ready to serve.

CHEFS NOTE

Try swapping the cocoa powder for your favourite branded hot chocolate powder for a bespoke taste.

OTHER COOKNATION TITLES

If you enjoyed I Love My Crepe Maker *you may also like other titles in the* **I♥MY** *series.*

To browse the full catalogue visit ***www.bellmackenzie.com***

Printed in Great Britain
by Amazon

36194479R00053